A Message to Santa

 Young**Writers**

First published in Great Britain in 2006 by:
Young Writers
Remus House
Coltsfoot Drive
Peterborough
PE2 9JX
Telephone: 01733 890066
Website: www.youngwriters.co.uk
All Rights Reserved
© *Copyright Contributors 2007*
SB ISBN13: 978-1-84602-844-1

Foreword

Our 'Poems for Santa' competition inspired many children to write about the magic of Christmas and the festive season: what they love about it and the excitement and fun it brings them. From Santa, Rudolph, roast turkey and tinsel to decorating the tree and ice skating, this anthology captures Christmas time and winter beautifully.

We are proud to present *A Message to Santa*. So much thought, effort and creativity has been put into each and every poem, and we enjoyed reading every single one. The task of selecting the overall winner was extremely enjoyable, but nevertheless a difficult task. You'll find the winner and runners-up at the front of this collection.

Young Writers was established in 1991 to promote poetry and creative writing to school children and encourage them to read, write and enjoy it. Here at Young Writers we are sure you'll agree that this fantastic edition achieves our aim and celebrates today's wealth of young writing talent. We hope you and your family continue to enjoy *A Message to Santa* for many years to come.

Contents

The Poems

Santa, Santa

Santa, Santa
Are you magic?
You like to ride in the midnight sky
Delivering presents to boys and girls
All over the big wide world

Santa, Santa
How old are you?
You must be at least 100 years
With your shiny red cheeks and long white beard

Santa, Santa
Is Rudolph's nose still shining bright
And does it light your sleigh at night?

Poor old Santa
Do you ever get tired?
I bet you sleep all Christmas Day
Snoring every hour away

Good old Santa we love you
I hope you get some presents too!

Patrick Bannister (9)

Winner!

Congratulations to Patrick, whose
prizewinning poem won him a fantastic
Christmas sack full of goodies which
was delivered in time for Christmas!

Hey Father Christmas

Hey Father Christmas
I have been good this year
So I hope that you can help me
If I make my wishes clear

Hey Father Christmas
I have been good this year
I'd like the world to be in peace
And wars to disappear

Hey Father Christmas
I have been good this year
I wish that children everywhere
Have food enough to share

Hey Father Christmas
I have been good this year
Give everyone a family
To love and care

Hey Father Christmas
I have been good this year
So I hope you'll help me
I made my wishes clear
I would just like one more thing
If it's not too much I fear
Could you and Rudolph possibly
Make a new bike appear?

Joshua Taylor (9)

My List To Santa

Dear Santa,

Can I have for Christmas ...
Lots of chocolate yum, yum, yum
That shiny handbag for my mum
Rainbow socks, very bright
A purple lamp for the night
The golden teddy with the furry nose
A pretty T-shirt and on the front a rose
That funny book I saw in York
A friendly doll that you can make talk
Those beautiful, shiny, gorgeous shoes
A lucky bracelet so I'll never lose
How many months, I know there is twelve
Oh and by the way, how are the elves?
Are they busy working, having fun,
Ready for the sleigh ride run?
How are the reindeer and Mrs Claus?
I hope she isn't mopping too many floors!
Most importantly, how are you?
Are you looking forward to a mince pie or two?

Love from
Francesca Harrison.

Francesca Harrison (10)

Runner -up
Francesca's poem won her a
Christmas stocking filled to
the brim with prizes.

Dreaming Of Christmas

All the stockings are hung on the wall,
waiting for him to arrive.
All of the children are tucked up in bed,
dreaming about Christmas Day.
The Christmas tree is decorated
with twinkling fairy lights.
As I dream about my presents
and think about Christmas dinner,
the sound of bells comes to my ears
as St Nicholas starts to deliver.
Down the chimney he comes
with his sack of presents.
He leaves them under the tree,
waiting for us to open them.
As he finishes his job,
he gets into his sleigh,
whacks the harness
and rides away.

Zoë Dunn (9)

Runner-up
Congratulations Zoë. You also
won a Christmas stocking filled
with prizes for your great poem.

The Christmas Wish

A teddy bear,
Some clothes to wear.
A candy cane,
A nice toy plane.
A bouncy ball,
Some chocolate is cool!
A paintball gun,
Board games are fun.
But ...
All I want from you this year,
Get ready to shout, ready to cheer,
It may sound a little bit sad,
But think about it, it's not that bad!
All I want is *love!*

Lauren Smith (10)

Christmas Day

Oh Christmas Day is a time of joy and merriness,
When I wake up, I feel the happiness.
I run down the creaky stairs
And see how much my family care.
I pull off the wrapping paper
And see a great present from my considerate neighbour.
Cookie crumbs on the plate,
Santa Claus must have thought they were absolutely great!
I get dressed in cosy clothes for Christmas Mass,
How quickly the year has come to pass!
After it is finished I go to my nanny's for Christmas dinner,
Her scrumptious food is definitely a winner!
I go back home and straight outside
And behind a bush to hide.
Scoop up a huge ball of freezing snow,
Still my brother doesn't know.
He opens the gate to look for me
And I grasp my snowball and fling it! He he he!
It comes to my bedtime,
Oh my poem does rhyme!
I pray to God thanking him for a tremendous day
And, 'That is no problem,' he does say.
My parents come and say goodnight
And I fall asleep until the morning light.

Harrison Fitzpatrick (10)

Untitled

I wake up, is it morning?
I see snow in the air.
I go downstairs into the living room
And see lots of presents there.

I hear a noise outside
I bravely sneak a look
And there is Santa on his sledge
With Rudolph eating nuts.

'Happy Christmas my darling,
I hope you like your presents.'
'Wait!' I shouted Santa.
'I have something special for you too.'
Mince pie, some hot chocolate
And a happy Christmas to you too.
With a blink of an eye and a dash of light
I waved my hand and said, 'Goodnight!'

Georgina Clay (8)

Untitled

Santa I've got a letter
I dearly hope you'll read
You see this letter
Means a lot to me

The Christmas tree and turkey
Isn't what Christmas is about
The presents help I'll admit
But of the meaning I have no doubt

'Cause I know you come every year
To children across the globe
Riding with your reindeer
In your recognisable crimson robe

So why do you do it Santa?
Because if what I've been taught is true,
You do it for the milk and cookies
But I refuse to believe that's you

Is your reasons for the stockings
Waiting to be filled
Or do you lean to the religious side
Jesus' birth memory being fulfilled?

'Cause if I was Santa I'd bring love
Is that what you do so well?
I'd bring peace and family to reunite
In a present wrapped in my spell

Like moss you've spread far and wide
Though some just won't believe
I know you're a good guy Santa
Won't you bring joy for me?

Kirsty May Mackmurdie (13)

16

Letter To Santa

Dear Santa,

This year I don't need presents
Toys and games or sweets
I don't want any make-up
Or festive chocolate treats

This year I need some magic
A small box filled with love
A message from the angels
Living high above

I also need my stocking
Brimming full of peace
A signal for all conflicts
And wars on Earth to cease

My Santa sack is filling
With happiness and joy
A smile for the rich and poor
Every girl and boy

Right underneath my tree
A large box filled with health
Cures every suffering person
Distributing our wealth

It's all I need for Christmas
A promise to all on Earth
To stop all hatred, cure all ills
On the day of Jesus' birth.

Annabelle Walker (17)

Poem For Santa

Santa, why do you fly in a sleigh?
Santa, why do you shout yey hey?
Why do you have reindeer to pull you?
Is it because you shout yahoo?

Santa, why do you drop off presents?
Is it because you want to be pleasant?
Why do you drop them down the chimney from so high?
Is it because you don't want to be spied?

Oh Santa, you're so funny!
Why do you dress in red?
Why not in blue or green
Or any other colour instead?

Selina Stoves (9)

Joyful Christmas Times

Snow is falling
Snow is falling upon the ground
Girls and boys are singing around

Santa, Santa is coming to town
All the children better be asleep
Or Santa won't be giving you presents to keep.

Chelsea Leigh (9)

On Christmas Eve

Santa, Santa is coming tonight
You better be asleep
You better be asleep
Or you will have no toys to keep!

Snow angels all around
Children can see snow angels on the ground
You better watch out!
You better beware!

Santa Claus is here, *shh, shh, shh!*

Megan James (9)

Christmas Poem

Shiny stars in the sky
Now it's Christmas
I wonder why
Jesus, Mary, Joseph too
What do they mean to me and you?

Children singing Christmas songs
Santa's coming, it won't be long
Special gifts under the tree
Some for you and some for me

Snowflakes, stockings, turkey too
Merry Christmas from me to you!

Dylan Bradley (7) & Lewis Fox (9)

Children Waiting!

On Christmas Eve night
The lights shine bright
Children waiting for Santa to come

On Christmas Day
The children play
With all their new toys
Merry Christmas!
Merry Christmas!

Cain Savage (7)

Dear Santa

Dear Santa,
Here is my poem about Christmas:
Christmas Day, Christmas Day,
Is a special holiday.
On Christmas Eve,
The elves all weave,
All our toys together!
Christmas hour, Christmas hour,
Is when you can get all the Christmas power.
On Christmas Day,
We might go away,
Or even stay at home!

Nicola Foss (10)

Poems for Santa

On Christmas Eve,
Santa Claus leaves
Us lots of different treats.
He gives us bears,
Which we cuddle and care
And he gives us lots of sweets.

Kriss Kringle
Gives us Pringles,
But he forgets to give us a dip!
He leaves us a toy,
Whether we're a girl or boy,
Then races home for a kip.

I wonder how he manages,
To do it all in a night,
No child has ever seen him,
Do it in their sight.

I wonder what Father Christmas
Wants as *his* present,
Maybe cookies and milk,
Or a coat made of silk,
Anyway he'd want something nice.

So on Christmas Eve,
I'll close my eyes,
Instead of looking to the skies.
Because if I look for him,
Through the stars,
He might forget that he needs to turn left at Mars!

Alice Cracknell (11)

Christmas Tree And Holly

Christmas tree, O Christmas tree
Turn on your lights for me
Christmas tree, O Christmas tree
Roast dinner for you and me
Christmas tree, O Christmas tree
Pressies under the tree
Christmas tree, O Christmas tree
Santa's stuck up a *chimney.*

Danielle Colvin (10)

The Santa Deception

Everyone was rushing,
No time for hushing,
All on Christmas Eve,
Santa was deceived.

His chief elf,
Mr Green,
Was in charge of Santa's health,
Among other things of clean.

Santa was so busy,
Making presents, seeing kids,
Santa started drinking and got a little dizzy,
He was drunk and started putting in bids.

When Santa got home,
He gnawed on a bone (chicken)
His wife had a shock,
As he tripped over a stone.

He hitched up the reindeer
And loaded the sleigh,
The little elves shout, anyone could hear,
The reindeer jumped and Santa shouted, 'Hey!'

Mr Green supposedly loaded the presents,
Santa hopped in and looked at the moon,
Its shape was a crescent
The sun would be rising, very soon.

He sped off to the north, the south, east and west,
But realised the presents weren't there,
Santa was not at his best,
He would simply have to run.

He raced back home,
He loaded the sacks,
He rushed back over the Millennium Dome,
No longer presents did he lack.

He delivered the presents to all different houses,
On and on, through the cold winter's night,
The sacks were piled high and full of surprises,
He even gave a lazy cat a fright.

At last, the night ended,
Everything done,
He went back home and lent
An elf a cosy pair of winter socks and they all had some fun.

They threw a party
And no matter what,
Everyone was very hearty
And everyone (especially Santa) drank a lot.

As they went to bed
Santa had a word,
With Mr Green
Who now has learned
No one messes with Santa and gets away with it.

Katherine Gilbert (11)

Is It You Santa?

I hear footsteps above me
pittering and pattering
a big thump underneath me
should I check who is there?

Maybe it's Santa
I get up out of bed
I wake up my mum
I wake up my dad
but nobody listens to me.

I sneak around
to the living room
who else but Santa giving gifts to me
I drop my mouth open and ask,

'Santa is that you?'
He turns around
he winks at me
he puts his finger on his lips and gives me a *shh*.

I run to my presents
he shouts, 'No!
Do you want to be on the naughty list again?'

I step back and I sigh
'I won't tell anyone if you don't.'
He laughs as loud as thunder
and disappears into thin air.

My mum calls me to go upstairs to bed
I turn around to say bye
but no one's there
I go upstairs to bed

I hear Santa's reindeer bells
look out my window and he waves.

Rachael Olatunbosun (11)

Cold Streets

The snow dances down,
Its paws grasping the ice-cold windows
The houses white as Everest
Doors as sad as the depressed man
Who lies there sulking, hopelessly, coldly
His tears turning to ice when they plunge heavily to the white pavement

Santa's sleigh crackles on
In the dark, lonely sky
He can only see the innocent houses
With their lights off, fire dead
No words
No movement

The parties start
Movement and noise begins
The noise ruins the calm atmosphere
Ends peace
Begins war
The fires crackle
The cups smash
All is well
Except Santa and the man

They are forgotten
Lost
Never noticed
No money is ever chucked at them
No generous, kind soul comes along
They just sit there
Helpless, lonely

Santa finishes
Pleased but not happy
He is worried about the man
Whose only purpose is to lie
Dry-mouthed, half dead
Hoping for at least a friendly soul to come
But there is something
A kind soul, walking along
Who knows the point of Christmas
To give everyone something
Even the man and Santa.

Louis A D Hall

Santa

S anta brings us presents
A nd never lets us down
N ot though if we're naughty
T hen we get some coal
A s my nana keeps telling me!

Jacqs Scourfield (10)

Santa Down The Chimney

I lay silently all through the night,
Then suddenly a *bump* to give me a fright,
I hear *bang, bang, bang* on the rooftops
Could it be Santa? Could it not?

I get to the stairs and I go down,
I go to the corner of the living room and see Santa with a frown,
He says, 'Ho, ho, no. I am stuck upside down,
If you help me out I will turn my frown around.'

I help Santa down,
I am glad to see presents,
'Ho, ho, ho,
I think I will give you more presents.'

I go back to bed,
Like nothing has happened,
I wonder if it was real
Or just made up.

Jade Rebecca Frances Crotty (9)

Poem For Santa

Santa is a brilliant man and the best,
He brings us lovely presents.
Santa has little elves to help him wrap the presents.
Dashing in the night,
Ready for us in the morning.

Lucy Hoskins (9)

Presents

Santa, please can you get me these,
They're only little things ...

A chocolate fountain,
A holiday with a snowy mountain,
A cuddly bear,
A massive, juicy watermelon (but not a pear),
A Bop It,
An Arsenal and England kit,
A gigantic bike,
A big trampoline (but I won't be able to do a pike),
A PSP,
A machine that makes tea!

That is all, but I have got more,
But I think I am being cheeky ...

Always remember I will be back next year!

Lauren Walsh (9)

Christmas

It's so exciting
Seeing everyone
Choosing their Christmas wish,
Seeing everyone kissing
Under the mistletoe,
Seeing tinsel and baubles on their Christmas tree,
The angels smiling and looking down at all the lovely gifts,
The fairies granting all the wishes over the village,
All the love is going all around on this particular day.
The holly is green and red hanging on the door,
The snowdrops are hanging with white snowy petals,
The presents are coloured red, white and blue in shiny paper.
Oh I love Christmas!

Charlotte Chamberlain (11)

Santa

S anta is big and red,
  he always wears a hat on his head.
A fter dark he gets on his sleigh,
  with his reindeer to pull him a long way.
N ight-time is when he's out,
  delivering presents that's what it's all about.
T racking through the ice and snow,
  he has a very long way to go.
A fter all the hard work is done,
  he goes home to bed and sucks his thumb.

Joshua Arthur (9)

Santa's Guide

On Christmas night
Rudolph's nose is bright
Santa and his reindeer fly into the skies
Santa hoping for mince pies
The reindeer will get a treat
Lots of crunchy carrots to eat.

Elliot Parker (10)

Oh Santa, Santa

Santa is on the roof
Whilst Christmas is here,
Another great season for us to cheer,
On this special day no one will jeer,
Because Santa is on the roof
Whilst Christmas is here.

Shannon Kooner (11)

Santa Claus

S is for the stocking on the chimney wall
A is for angels who tell people things
N is for the noise of all the Christmas cheer
T is for the toys under the Christmas tree
A is for the apples roasting on an open fire

C is for candy on the Christmas tree
L is for the love with everyone
A is for the acrobats performing on the stage
U is for the children unwrapping presents
S is for the spirit which makes people happy, for everyone who helps make Christmas fun.

Sophie Morgan (8)

Dear Cameron

I'm sorry I can't bring the purple dinosaur,
But it really won't fit through your tiny front door.
I won't be able to get you a motorbike,
Mummy says you should really get a trike.
You can't have a rock climbing kit,
Daddy's afraid the helmet won't fit.
You can't have a plane,
Argos say they're out of stock,
Instead I'll get you a very nice clock.
I won't get you a panther,
I'm sorry,
From
Santa.

PS See what happens next year!
Maybe then I'll get a cheer!

Elinor Simms (10)

Santa

Santa walks through your tiles,
He gives you presents with a smile,
He tiptoes past your room,
He tiptoes past the other room,
Then he climbs up the chimney with great care,
Then he walks to his sleigh
And then he goes where?

He goes to a house,
With no mouse!

Ian Mercado (10)

Dear Santa Claus

I don't understand
Why I can't see you
Or even hold your hand,
Why didn't you eat the cookies
I left out for you last night?
If I'd only heard your reindeer
I wouldn't have got a fright
And why didn't I find any footprints in the snow?
Surely you have to be real,
So why weren't there any to show?
Oh please, Santa, please,
You have to be real,
You know?

Shannon Kennedy (11)

Untitled

There's someone on the roof
going stomp, stomp, stomp!
There's someone in the chimney
going cough, cough, cough!
There's someone in our living room
by our tree.
Who could it be,
Santa maybe?

Charlotte King (11)

Santa Claus

S is for *S*anta all cheerful and proud
A is for Santa will be *a*round
N is for he will *n*ever let you down
T is for *t*reats all big and small
A is for *a*ddresses he needs to know

C is for *C*hristmas all aglow
L is for *l*ove and peace
A is for *a*wesome flying reindeer
U is for *u*nique powers
S is for *s*mile gleaming and white.

Sian Gibbs (11)

Untitled

Christmas Eve waiting for you
It takes a long time, I don't know what to do
Staring out the window, looking at the stars
I know you're faster than any car
I start to get tired, my eyes start to close
But when I wake up I'll have the toys that I chose.

Connor Walters (7)

Santa's On His Way!

Hello Santa
Are you ready
To go on your sleigh,
I hope you're steady.

I wonder what you have
Inside your sack,
Maybe full of surprises
Carrying on your back.

Going down the chimney
Is really fun,
But if you're caught
You better make a run.

At last you have finished
Delivering all the presents,
When everyone has woken up
I hope they are pleasant!

Sabina Haneefa (11)

Dear Santa ...

Dear Santa,
I hope you think that I have been
A very good girl this year,
I've left a mince pie just for you
And a carrot for your deer.
Sorry, we're out of sherry,
So I had to leave you beer
And when I hear your sleigh bells ring,
I promise not to peer.

I really want a Barbie doll
So I can brush her hair
And dress her up in pretty clothes
And take her everywhere!

And I would like a painting set
So I can draw my dad,
I'd hang his picture on the wall,
To cheer me when I'm sad.

I really want a new CD,
I really, really do,
All my friends have got one
And I wish I had one too.

I won't ask you for a pony,
It won't fit in your sleigh,
But whatever gifts you bring me,
I'll enjoy Christmas Day.

Lottie Taylor (11)

My Emotions At Christmas

My emotions at Christmas are hard to explain,
It's like taking a ride on a big aeroplane.

I am very excited and mostly delighted,
I hope Santa comes but he hasn't been sighted.

He started his journey from a very long way,
He's heading for me on his bright big red sleigh.

My butterflies I get are not over yet,
I'm jumping with glee to see what's for me.

But I know if I don't get nothing at all,
I won't sit and cry, shout or bawl
Because I know I've got the best family of all.

So here's something I'm desperate to say,
Merry Christmas and have a good day!

Hayley Mitchell (9)

My Christmas Wish List

Dear Santa,
For Christmas may I have
An Xbox 360,
A PS3,
Or maybe a Nintendo Wii?
I hope I haven't been too naughty,
Because plainly you can see;
I've eaten the sprouts on my dinner
And cabbage on my tea.
I've washed my dad's car
And walked the dog way too far.
I'll leave you sherry and a mince pie
Because I think you're a great guy.

Sasha Wood (11)

Dear Santa

Dear Santa,
I've waited so many years to say,
How can you eat all those cookies in one night
And stay the same way?
Now I don't ask for a lot,
But here's another question too,
Would you be with me even if I was in Peru?
I may not be a perfect kid,
I've heard my parents say,
But would you give me a special gift on Christmas Day?
Would you visit me if I was an alien?
What about a cat?
Would you even visit me if I was bitten by a bat?
So what about it Santa
Presents or what?
The least I ask of my presents is a *wicked* robot
And not an evil one like last year!

From you know who!

Hannah Grafton (11)

Christmas Eve

Crackers popping
Children hopping
Tinsel glittering
Baubles sparkling
Children laughing
Trees glowing
Presents wrapping
Santa's coming
Children snoring.

Aaron Molyneux (10)

Untitled

Christmas Eve is drawing near,
the day Santa flies with his reindeer.
I hang my stocking on the wall
and hope the next day it will be full.
I lay a mince pie on the table
and hope that he will be able
to eat it up
and drink his milk from the cup.
If you do these things yearly,
Santa will give you the things you want dearly.

Paige Lamb (9)

Christmas

C old wintry night
H uddles up in bed
R ise up in the morning
I n a good mood
S anta has been
T o give us gifts
M erry Christmas everyone!
A nd have a good rest
S anta.

Michael Sandison Yeoman (10)

Dear Santa

It's nearly Christmas time
And I hope you're feeling fine,

The North Pole must be cold
Especially when you're old,

Get your reindeer ready
And fly across the sky

I will get you a beer
And a mince pie,

The time has come
For us to have fun,

Hooray, Christmas Day is here
And we all shout and cheer,

Presents under the tree
And a sack from you to me,

I do love *Christmas* it's such fun
And thank you Santa from everyone.

Joel Manning (9)

St Nicholas' Journey

His sack is lined with presents,
In the colours blue, pink and green,
His clothes are red and white,
With soot-black boots, tied up tight.

Climbing off his sleigh,
Giving carrots to his reindeer,
It's night whereas on the other side of the world it is day.
Santa slips down the chimney with a *bang,*
This wasn't in the plan!

He sees the Christmas tree,
As brightly lit as could be.
Placing the presents in great presentation,
Beneath the baubles and behind the Nativity,
Beside the gifts lies a note from Santa himself.

Worded in exceptional English,
For someone who comes from Lapland
Santa is someone you may never meet,
However he is full of Christmas cheer!

Maisie McCormack (11)

Santa Claus

S anta is so full of cheer, at this festive time of year
A cross the world he flies at night
N icely giving presents before the morning light
T eddies, bikes, balls, kites and goodness knows what else
A ll fill his sleigh, on this winter's night

C rashing through the snow, his reindeer fly
L ike thunderbolts, across the sky
A nother year has flown by
U nder the stars, Santa does fly
S leeping children dream of a winter wonderland where,
 elves make toys and the air is filled with Christmas cheer.

Georgina Biggar (8)

Dear Santa

For Christmas I want a family
Who'll really love me so,
Who'll hold my hand when I'm really down,
Who'll watch me as I grow.

For Christmas I want a friend,
We'll play endless games together,
She will have long hair and a pretty face
And she'll help if I'm under the weather.

For Christmas I want to be loved
So that my life could change,
But no one wants a girl like me
Who's cold, alone and strange.

I really want this, Santa,
Honestly, I really would,
I promise I'll be a good girl
If only you actually could.

Rema Farhan (11)

Hi Santa!

I think it would look rude asking for presents,
So I made a list of what *you* want!

Would you like some mince pies?
No, some mulled wine?
A carrot for Rudolph,
A CD for Dancer,
Some ballet shoes for Dasher and Prancer!

What about an iPod,
To download the Christmas tunes,
Or a 42-inch plasma screen,
To watch 'Santa Clause 2'?
But are you an electrical person?

I could make you a jam tart,
Or a winter casserole,
Or a frothy, creamy hot cocoa!

I thought maybe a *red,* warm parka coat,
With matching *red* gloves and scarf,
For walking round the North Pole,
Or would you prefer blue?

I then thought of a more *special* gift,
A candle on a piece of wood,
With holly leaves, tinsel and snowflakes,
Wrapped up with some personalised paper,
Placed under your pretty tree
And guess what? They're all made by me!

So Santa when you look under your tree on Christmas Day,
Look for the present that's special,
That's your present from me!

Ellen Turner (11)

Santa Is Coming

Santa is coming
With his big red sack
Filled to the brim with all the toys inside

While all the children are in bed, fast asleep
Santa delivers all the joyful treats

Jingle, jangle go his big sleigh bells
Over the mountains and very far away.

Kymani Armstrong-Williams (7)

Dear Santa

I wanted to write a poem just for you
I would write my name at the bottom but you would think, *who*?
So I am writing you this poem and it's going to be fab
And you'll know my name isn't something silly like Bab
I'll hang up my stocking on Christmas Eve
And when I open a present I'll leave a holly leaf
I'll go to sleep before you arrive
And snore really loud so you know I'm alive
I'll leave you a card made by me
And you'll know that I'm a 'she' and not a 'he'

So Santa that is it, my poem for you
And I hope you no longer look and think, *who?*
But wait, before you go, I've left you
And Mrs Christmas some *mistletoe!*

Rachel Moscrop (10)

What's Christmas?

What does it look like?
It looks like a newborn puppy or like the first smile of a baby.
What does it smell like?
It smells like fresh snow or like candles that have just been blown out.
What does it taste like?
It tastes like hot chocolate by the warm fire
or like freshly cooked Christmas pudding with warm custard.
What does it sound like?
It sounds like the rustling of wrapping paper when a child
opens its first present or like the laugh of a baby playing.
But what it reminds me most of is the moment
my baby brother was born.
So that is what Christmas looks, smells, tastes and sounds like
and what it reminds me most of.
So remember that forever and ever!

Caitlin Budding (10)

When Santa's On His Way ...

The lights are all turned off.
Everyone's in bed, as silent as mice.
Just waiting for the mysterious man dressed in red,
to climb down the sooty, black chimney.
Thud!
He hits the ground with a great bang.
Then lays the pretty ribbon presents under the tall, graceful tree.
Wrapped carefully in red and gold.
He climbs up the chimney with a great force.
He sits in his sleigh and sends the reindeer away.

April Buxton (11)

All I Want For Christmas

All I want for Christmas is a PSP,
Would you be kind enough to please get one for me?

I've been well behaved this year,
I've done all my chores and stayed away from my mum's beer.

All I want is to see that big red parcel in front of that huge green tree,
The morning after you have magically slipped down my chimney.

Your big black sack full to the top,
I hope at my house a present you'll drop.

All I want for Christmas is a PSP,
Would you be kind enough to please get one for me?

Hannah Jayne Thomas (13)

I've Been Good

Santa, Santa I hope you come
Will you bring presents for everyone?
I'll lay out a mince pie and maybe some wine
I'll put out a massive sign
Now I will go to bed and listen to what my mummy said
Our Christmas tree is ready
I hope I'll get a teddy.
From
Leanne.

Leanne Bastick (9)

Christmas Time

Christmas time, Christmas time
Presents, Santa, gifts
Christmas time, Christmas time
A mistletoe kiss

Christmas time, Christmas time
Hats, scarves and snow
Christmas time, Christmas time
Seeing people you know

Christmas time, Christmas time
Eating for lunch big roasts
Christmas time, Christmas time
Receiving lots of Christmas post

Christmas time, Christmas time
Christ's birthday
Christmas time, Christmas time
So let's all say ...
'Happy birthday!'
On this special day.

Caitlin Gerry (9)

Santa

A small poem from me to you,
I hope you enjoy it,
Thanks for all the joy you bring,
To every little child throughout

S   is for special,
A   is for amazing,
N   is for nice,
T   is for terrific,
A   is for all you stand for

C   is for your curly, cloudy beard,
L   is for your laughing face,
A   is for your adorable reindeer,
U   is for your unique, ultra sleigh,
S   is for your small, sweet elves.

Joe K Strachan (10)

Santa's Presents

What would you give Santa?
A pair of comfy slippers,
Or some swimming flippers,
A bottle of wine,
A new watch to tell the time.

What would you give Santa?
Scrumptious little chocs,
All wrapped up in a box,
Scented bubble bath,
A toy to make him laugh.

What would you give Santa?
A new bright red coat,
Or a pet billy goat,
A woolly hat or a cricket bat.

What would you give Santa?
Candy cane tasty and sweet,
So nice and good to eat.
A night cap all warm and snug
Ready for a bedtime hug.

What would you give Santa?
The latest DVD
Or top ten chart CD,
A nice new book
To teach him how to cook.

What would you give Santa?

Heather Seldon (9)

Santa Claus

Santa Claus
Can't pause
Because he is a busy man
Mr Santa Claus if you wanna know I'm your biggest fan
He has many names
He loves to play games
He had walked upon many lanes
And he loves to walk near Thames
He travels around the world in one day
He starts making toys in May
He hasn't got time to lay
But he never forgets to pray
He is so busy
But he never gets dizzy
He hates to travel in the mist
And some call him Chris.

Nishali Karunatilleke (9)

The Elves

The elves' work is almost done, soon it will be Christmas fun,
Every day and every hour they've been using their elf power.
On Christmas Eve Santa can't wait to leave,
Our presents that we will receive
Under the little Christmas tree as soon as can be.
They work for love and not for pay
To hear the worlds that you will say,
Rudolph with your nose so bright,
You're like a little shining light
To guide Santa through the night.
Santa we do adore, bring us presents more and more.
Ho, ho, ho, merry Christmas!

Chloe Yates (11) & Bradley Yates (8)

Joy Of Christmas

Rudolph hobbles,
On the cold, frozen cobbles,
The wind whistles through a tree,
As my mum drinks her morning tea.

Santa tiptoes by,
As fireworks light the sky,
Christmas lights turn on everywhere,
As we hear wrapping paper tear.

Carol singers singing so jolly,
As we make our way through spiky holy,
The moon shines ever so brightly,
As I tug on my scarf tightly.

It's Christmas time
And all is fine!

Abigail Hansford (11)

Santa's Shadow

Leafless trees lean and quiver,
A golden fox darted past with a shiver.
But all not in fear,
For a kind-hearted fellow was approaching near.
Some call him old Saint Nick or Santa Claus,
By the fur-coated animals and children indoors.
His wispy, whirly beard, blood-red coat and bushy eyebrows white,
Please all, even the shadows in the pitch-black night.
He brings widespread smiles and all things dark to dazzling light.
A worn brown sack slung over his shoulder,
Excites smiling children as the warm fire smoulders.
A large, leather belt fastened across his satin coat, with golden trim-
ming,
Matches his sack, with great gifts brimming.
That old kindly face, with raisin eyes,
Is invaded with magic, happiness and surprise.

Selina Donophy (11)

Poem For Santa

When I wake on Christmas morn,
I'd like to find,
Not the usual presents
Of the usual kind,
For although I take great pleasure
In the gadgets, gizmos and toys,
I know a present that I'm more likely to enjoy.
So this year, when you fill my stocking again,
Please put in it peace on Earth and goodwill to men.

Joanna Moberly (10)

Christmas Time

Christmas spirit,
Christmas cheer,
It's everybody's favourite time of year,
So don't be miserable,
Don't be sad,
It's Christmas time, there's fun to be had,
Wrap up presents,
Send them to your friends,
It will all be worth it in the end.

Sheneece Brooks (10)

Christmas

C is for the children playing with the snow all day
H is for the houses covered with the glowing lights
R is for the reindeer flying really, really high
I is for the icing on the Christmas cake today
S is for the stocking filled with sweets as sweet as sugar cane
T is for the tinsel on the merry Christmas tree
M is for the many presents that we all receive
A is for the Advent calendar counting down the days
S is for the snowman standing in the cold, hooray!

Callan Danvers (10)

Dear Santa

I simply just felt you should know
That sometime a week or two ago
I saw one of your trusted elves misbehaving
Misbehaving right there on my roof

He was *ranting and raving,* shouting *out many things*
And everyone wondered what was happening
'For a fee and a pledge, you can ride Santa's sledge'
A promise we knew he could never keep

Now I'm guessing you'll be needing a speedy replacement
Someone passionate about this annual event
Who marvels and gasps at the seasonal delights
And at night prays for peace in the world

Well have no fear, there is someone right here
Who is ready to step in those shoes
Someone fit for the part, with the right sort of heart
And a very good head for heights

I can tell you I work very hard in school
And at home, I follow every rule
I practise my instrument every day
And eat cabbage and porridge without fuss

So please choose me to be an elf this Christmas
And I surely will do my best
I will do what elves do and won't stop till I'm through
And the rest ... well it's all up to you!

From
Stephanie.

Stephanie Hanson (9)

Untitled

Counting down the days
keeping my good ways
hoping that he'll come
so I can have some fun

dreaming of a horse
take it on an off road course
I'm wondering what he'll bring
could it be a diamond ring?

Do my cards
make the cake
wrap the presents
and stay up late

six o'clock
nice and early
jump on Mum.

Louise Nash (12)

Santa

Sleigh rider
Sky glider

Red wearer
Reindeer carer

Elf owner
Present donor

Ho-ho-ho!
It's ... *Santa!*

Heather Louise Wilson (8)

A Poem For Santa

Santa Claus, are you really true?
Once you came and your reindeer too.
Is there really a gift that comes from you
For me, my sister, my mom and dad too?

My sister likes dolls, they give her a smile
And I love a car that runs a mile.
Don't worry about my mom and my dad,
I'm making a card that I'm sure they will love.

I always pray to see you,
To hug and thank you,
For all the gifts you gave me before
And for the other gifts you will give me more.

Adrien Joshua F Guiking (9)

Santa Claus

Santa Claus is here again
Come let's celebrate again
With the witty pot-belly
Gleaming white huge beard
Wedded to his flattering jaw;
Dome flesh and soft buttock
Clothed in a deep red damask
Laced with scanty shiny white cloth,
His clowning shoe evokes a yuletide
Sarcastic laughter from the mouth
Of every child during Christmas time.

Santa Claus is here again
Come let's celebrate again
Oldies and yuppies in the train
Like the bubbles in the train.
The fun is quite unlimited
In this season of pun stead,
Harmony flourishes in happiness and cheers.
Come let's wine and dine with peers
At the amazing amusement parks
The age-long home of Santa Claus!

Aderemi Adegbite

Who Am I?

He goes around, all in red,
Carries something on his back.
When we're in bed,
He empties his sack.

He lands on our roofs,
With a great clatter,
Whilst the reindeer hooves,
Make quite a patter.

Down the chimney he goes,
Trying to make himself small.
Then, a problem arose,
So he began to bawl.

'Help!' he cried. 'I'm stuck up here!
Rudolph where are you?
It's too much Christmas beer!'
'Oh no! What can we do?'

Rudolph pulled and hurt his nose,
Instead of red, it went blue!
He finally got him free, the story goes,
So he can give presents to you.

We know who he is.
Do you?

Laura Scott (10)

Santa's Journey

From the North Pole,
Santa loads all his stuff
And sets off with his reindeer
Through the mountains and rough

He goes over Australia
Indonesia, New Guinea
Gets a new tie in Thailand
And then stops at India

He goes around Africa
And stops in Cape Town
Then heads north
To where a lady has a crown

He heads over Europe
As it is nearly morning
Flies over the Atlantic
As the day is dawning

He goes through New York
In the USA
Heads south to Brazil
And gets a burger on the way

Into the jungle
Through the trees
He zooms to the north
Away from the bees

The North Pole is quiet
There's not even a peep
Santa's in bed
And he's gone to sleep.

Luke Stothard (11)

Christmas Hooray

It's Christmas Day,
Hooray, hooray!
It's started to snow,
Hooray, hooray!
Has Santa been?
Let's take a peek,
Yes he has,
Hooray, hooray, hooray!
It's Christmas Day.

Jack Rhodes (6)

'Tis The Season

A tree with tinsel and baubles,
A snowman with a carrot for a nose,
Santa with a beard so snowy white and all his big red clothes.
The stockings are hanging by the fire,
Rudolph and the other reindeer are all ready to pull the sleigh,
The presents are wrapped and Santa's on his way,
To make every girl and boy's Christmas a very special day.

Emily Rhodes (10)

Dear Santa

I would like snow on Christmas Eve,
Whilst helping my mum to decorate the tree.
A roaring fire, mince pies, mulled wine,
While Christmas carols are sung all the time.
We put up the stockings 1, 2, 3,
I hope Santa leaves a surprise for me.
Off to bed, no sleepy head,
'Ho, ho, ho,' someone said.
I think I hear jingle bells as I drift off, oh sleepy head.

Charlotte Rhodes (11)

Christmas Surprises!

C is for Christ who was born this day and the shooting star that led the way
H is for holidays and no homework from school
R is for the red-nosed reindeer who pulls Santa's sleigh
I   is for the incense, that sweet smell I love
S is for the snowmen wrapped in hat and gloves
T is for the toboggan which is waiting to be used
M is for the mistletoe which my brothers put up in hope
A is for the angels watching over us
S is, at last, for old Santa Claus who I hear but never see

S is for the snowflakes tickling my nose and freezing my toes
U is for the unpleasant vegetables which are put on our plates (yuck)
R is for the other reindeer who fly all through the night
P is for the presents who are from you and me
R is for rejoice! When the Saviour is born
I   is for the ice which is so slippereee,
S is for the sweets which my nan gives to me
E is for the enormously decorated tree and, at last
S is for old Santa Claus who has just visited me!

Gabriella Crawford (10)

Dear Santa

What I want this Christmas,
Is very dear to you,
A very merry Christmas
And a happy New Year too.

You can get me loads of presents,
That will make me smile,
But when you come to town,
That will make me wild.

I bet those Elves are tired
And I bet you are too.
Rudolph the red-nosed reindeer,
I hope your aren't blue.

Christmas morning is here, hip hip hooray.
Open all my presents
And see Santa's sleigh,
Riding through the sky.

Laura Cambridge (11)

My Christmas Day

Early morning I open my eyes,
hope Santa's been, eaten his mince pies,
slowly I open my bedroom door,
wonder how many presents, one, two, maybe more.

I go and wake my mum and dad,
I know he's been, I've been a good lad,
we all go downstairs one step at a time,
I see all the gifts ... are they all mine?

I run to the pile and rip off some paper,
just what I wanted, my favourite, Darth Vader,
before I know it they're all undone,
I really did have so much fun.

Now to see what I really got,
my oh my there's quite a lot,
Mum goes to cook Christmas dinner,
turkey, stuffing, sprouts, together are a winner,

So my Christmas Day comes to an end as you know,
only another 364 days to go!

Kieran Gillott (7)

Tell Me Why, Santa

Dear Santa,

Tell me why you have a big red nose
And why you have wiggly toes.
Tell me why you ride a sleigh
And why Christmas isn't in May.
Tell me why you have a beard
And why you aren't feared.
Tell me why you have a hat
And why you're so fat.
Tell me why you don't wear green
And why you don't have a team.
Tell me why you don't wear yellow
And why you're so mellow.

Sophie Crockett (13)

Winter

Winter is the time of year when you ...

Open your presents,
But your mum says it's too early.

Make a snowman
But your mum says it's too cold.

Decorate the Christmas tree,
But your mum says you're too short.

Go ice skating,
But your mum says it's too slippery.

Eat turkey,
Now I say, that's more like it.

Jake Pomfret (9)

Santa Claus

S anta sweeps down the chimney on Christmas Eve
A nd a lot of presents for children he leaves
N ice presents for the good and coal for the bad
T o have coal would make me sad!
A nd so I'll be as good as gold

C hristmas is coming, the tree stands tall
L ast minute rushes to the mall
A n excited Santa hurries about preparing his sleigh
U nder the covers I dream about Christmas Day
S anta Claus goes merrily on his way.

Casey-Leigh Watkins (12)

The Magic Christmas Box

(Based on 'Magic Box' by Kit Wright)

In the box I will put ...

The merry jingle of Christmas bells,
The smile of a happy child
And a special Christmas wish.

In the box I will put ...

The twelve days of Christmas,
A ruby-red berry from a holly wreath
And the excited thumps of reindeer hooves
On a magical Christmas Eve.

In the box I will put ...

The jolly laugh of Santa Claus,
A beautiful snow dome
With glittering snowmen and snowflakes
And a sprinkle of crisp marzipan from a Christmas cake.

My box is fashioned from gold
And gleaming ice and snow,
With holly tangling the hinges
And snowdrops on the padlock.

Molly Masters (9)

Santa

He leaves presents under your tree
I wonder who it could be
I hear Christmas bells ringing
And someone singing
I hear tapping on my roof
It sounds like reindeer hooves
Who is this mysterious person?
Ah I know ... *Santa*.

Sam Bullock (10)

Santa's Grotto

Wow!
I walk in, blink twice,
Candy canes and chocolate mice.
Every colour you can see,
Everything looks good to me.
I stop, I stare, I twirl around,
Listen carefully to every sound.
Christmas tunes fill the air,
I sing along without a care.
Laughter here and giggles there,
All these things I'd love to share.
I walk further, through a door,
Toys and sweets and fun galore.
I step outside on white crisp snow,
A bright red bag with golden bow.
It sits snug, on Santa's sleigh,
All these things for Christmas Day.
Presents, presents, for me and you,
Thank you Santa, we love you too!

Emma Hall (14)

Awake

This year I will stay awake
I will not sleep or dream
I will stay awake till Santa's been
I'll stay awake
I'll stay awake and take a peep
Before I get some decent sleep
I will not sleep
I will not slumber
Not let my heavy eyelids clo- ...
Not let ...
My ...
Eyelids ...
Close.

James McLear (10)

It's Christmas Eve

Santa Claus is on his way,
Getting ready for Christmas Day,
He is very excited, all merry and jolly,
As we hang up the Christmas holly.

His cloak is red, his beard is white,
How does he deliver it all in just one night?
Remote control cars, teddies
And oh this and that,
How does Saint Nicholas fit it all
In that big fat sack?

I check my stocking,
It is full of presents all for me,
I look at the clock happily,
But it is only half-past three.

Morning *at last*
I'll see what he's brought,
A new bike for me?
Just as I thought.

Jordan Criddle (11)

Christmas Time

Rise and shine
Loads of presents and cards
Father Christmas comes
From down the chimney
For his yummy mince pies
And of course the pressies
The lovely pressies
With our dreams inside!

Laisha Mansfield (9)

Santa's Watching

Listen up kids I'm giving you a shout,
Christmas is coming, Santa's watching
So you better watch out.
If you want to wake up with presents under the tree,
Please be good, that's coming from me.
The bells are ringing, the angels are singing,
Look forward to the presents that Santa is bringing.
You'll find out something that you'll really want to know,
I'm telling you to be good so don't say no.
So remember what I've told you,
A message from me, don't forget Santa's coming
Yip, yip, yippee!

Shannice Chinnery (8)

Dear Santa

For me a candy cane,
A rabbit that isn't insane,
A new set of gloves and hats,
Please don't give me any rats,
I tried not to be naughty,
I can count to forty,
Oh, please forgive me,
If it's not what you usually see.

I'll leave you a mince pie,
A glass of sherry that isn't dry,
I'd love to see an elf,
I would wait for him by myself,
I won't tell a soul,
Try not to get full of coal,
I'll go fast asleep
And try not to peep.

Ella Clarkson (10)

Christmas

Santa, Santa where is your sleigh,
Is it bringing presents for Christmas Day?
Lots of presents for girls and boys,
Bringing peace and happiness to the world
On Christmas day hip hip hooray!

Bethany Chapman (10)

My Christmas Poem

C arols are sung
H uge presents to be opened
R oast dinners eaten
I ngredients in big dinners
S now all around
T welve days of Christmas
M erry times
A mounts of money spent
S ing songs.

Jordan Mead (9)

Father Christmas

Poor Father Christmas,
He only has working days,
He wraps up all the things he's made,
That's his working ways.

Thank you Father Christmas
Each Christmas Eve we think of you,
You have to get down the chimney,
How do you get through?

So, Father Christmas once that is done,
You see a huge glow, oh no! It's the sun.
Quickly Father Christmas, you must fly high
Back to the North Pole in the sky.

Zoe Boniface (9)

Santa, Santa

Santa, Santa delivering my presents when the year is through,
On his sleigh with Rudolph too!
Stepping across the silent snow,
Making not a sound on tiptoe.
Putting the presents under the tree,
For the children to see!

Georgia Leyland (8)

Santa's Coming Tonight

All the children tucked in bed,
Listening for Santa's sleigh,
Hoping for lots of presents in the morning,
Every house that Santa stops at
He gets mince pies and a glass of milk.
Sometimes he even thinks he will get
Too fat to go down the chimney!

Katie Alkaradi (9)

Down The Chimney

Down came Santa Claus
Down from the chimney
His cheeks rosy red and his nose like a berry
He wore bright red clothes
But they were covered in soot
And on his back was a big black sack
It was as big as him and filled to the brim
Gifts to be adored by children of all ages
But nothing compares to the smiles on our faces.

Erin Houston (10)

Santa Is A Man

Santa is a man
Who needs a frying pan
Santa is a man
Who's got a so-called clan

Santa is a man
Who drinks from Coke cans

Santa is a man
Who gets told off by Nan

Santa is a man
As if he needs a fan

Santa is a man
That really needs a tan

That is Santa.

Adam Parsons (11)

Santa

Your beard is pearly white
Your spectacles shimmer in the moonlight
Your coat is white and red
You visit us when we're in bed
You give us presents once a year
You put the presents under a tree
Then you say goodbye
To make every smile cheer
Even if you aren't a bird
You still can fly
Through the night's starry sky
Santa you are the jolliest man ever.

Emma Moorhouse (7)

When Does Santa Come?

He comes in the night!
He comes in the night!
He softly and silently comes.

While little brown heads
On pillows of white,
Are dreaming of bugles and drums.

He cuts through the snow
Like a ship through the foam,
While the little, white snowflakes swirl.

Who tells him? No one knows!
But he finds the bedside
Of each good boy and girl.

He comes in the night!
He comes in the night!
He softly and silently comes.

Jessica Davidson (9)

It's Nearly Christmas

Christmas is near
It's getting colder
Santa Claus is coming
To bring you lots of presents
Write your Christmas list
Quickly think of your Christmas list
Have you been a good girl or boy?
It is getting colder
Put your stockings up!

Tiegan Taylor-Helm (8)

Santa

Dear Santa,

I don't want a lot for Christmas,
Only the biggest thing you can buy!
If I don't get it I will die!
I need something special,
I'm making this wish,
I really don't want a fish.
But all I'm asking Santa please, please, please,
I'm begging you down on my knees,
I really would be pleased if you could get me a trapeze,
This Christmas Santa, please,
Or I might sneeze!
I really am down on my knees,
I would really love a trapeze!

Vikki Newbert (10)

Untitled

Take a bite of a turkey breast
and some stuffing.
Watch the reindeer fly over the sky
huffing and puffing.
'Go to bed,' that's what Mum said,
'and you'll get presents in the morning.'

Chloe Little (9)

There He Goes

'Ho, ho, ho!'
Through the night, that's all you hear,
In his sleigh led by reindeer.
You go to bed,
With a grin and a smile,
Wondering if the milk and cookies
Will make it worthwhile.
There's presents under the tree
And you think, *is that one for me?*

The night is almost done as you glare in the sky
And you wonder, *will Santa ever say hi?*
All you hear is, 'Ho, ho, ho.'
Now that the night is done
And there he goes!

Tevan Hudson (12)

Father Christmas

Father Christmas,
Father Christmas,
You travel north, south, east and west!
Father Christmas, Father Christmas,
I suggest you have a rest!
I have told no lies
And I will give you mince pies,
So please leave me a surprise!

Natascha Ng (8)

Santa's Coming

Santa's coming
Ho, ho, ho
With lots of presents
For me and you
With a big fat belly
And a nose aglow
Santa's coming
Ho, ho, ho.

Shannon McNulty (10)

Christmas Time

The bells are ringing,
Carollers are singing,
You can hear the sound
Of your microwave pinging,
With your Christmas pudding inside,
Yum!

Snow is falling,
The day is dawning,
As a red star shines.
There it goes
Whizzing past!
As the reindeer go riding.

It's the time of day,
Hip hip hooray!
Because Santa Claus is calling!
Ho, ho, ho!
Merry Christmas!

Jessica Perks (11)

Presents Galore!

Presents galore, presents galore,
Ask for anything you want,

Presents galore, presents galore,
Maybe a present hunt?

Presents galore, presents galore,
Around the Christmas tree,

Presents galore, presents galore,
They make your heart fill with glee!

Priya Kaur (10)

Untitled

What should I put on my Christmas list tonight?
A dragon's tooth from China town
Or what about a clumsy clown?
A nasty witch's evil hat?
Maybe a beautiful black and white cat?
That shall do,
Or should I add another thing or two?
I could write down a fairy's wing,
But I could write down Sweden's king.
What about a great white shark
Or a naughty yappy Jack Russell's bark?
I think that might be everything,
Let's hope that's what Santa will bring!

Rebecca Shiner (11)

Christmas

On Christmas Eve I go to bed
I slowly rest my sleepy head
Santa comes, with Rudolph and all
Down the chimney, with a great fall
He puts the gifts under the tree
All for me and my family
In my kitchen, there lies his treat
I have left for him, something sweet
Then off he goes in a hurry
He'll make it in time, don't worry
On Christmas Day I wake up early
Mum gets up, her hair is all curly
We all go downstairs together
Like we've always done, forever

We all run over, to see what's under the tree
Lots of big presents for me and my family!

Amy Lewtas (13)

Dear Santa

You may think I'm naughty,
Just because I fight,
But you are wrong
And I am right,

I know I scare kids
And hurt cats and mice
And yell at the teachers,
Even though they are nice,
But I am as good, as good as can be,
So bring lots of presents straight to me.

Katy Summers (10)

Can I Be You For A Day?

Dear Santa,

Can I be you for a day?
Maybe on the fourth of May,
I want to be you
Because I love making presents and giving them too.
This year I filled a box for children who are poor,
I like to give them lots from your store.
But if you say no then do me this wish,
Give everyone gifts and food on their dish.

Love
Eleanor.

Eleanor Wetherilt (11)

Dear Santa

I am sitting beside the Christmas tree,
Wondering about all the things to be.
Next to the Christmas tree
There is a present from you to me.
In the present next to the Christmas tree
I hope you remembered a teddy especially for me.

PS Did you enjoy the mince pie I gave you?

Eve Pilley (7)

Christmas

C hristmas is a time of year which brings happiness and cheer
H ouses are decorated with colourful lights
R eindeer flying about all night
I cing the cake on Christmas Eve
S nowflakes dancing all through the night
T rees are looking pretty and bright
M erry Christmas, the choirs all chorus
A fter Christmas all the decorations are being put away
S anta will come another day.

Molly Heeger (10)

Santa

Santa calls but once a year,
Children's faces full of cheer.

Presents a-plenty for girls and boys,
Only good children get his toys.

Reindeer ready, sleigh to load,
Places to visit in every road.

Snow is falling, lights all bright,
Santa's got a busy night.

So all you children, girls and boys,
Wishing for all your Christmas toys,
Off to bed, an early night.

Then wait for morning, a wondrous sight!

Jack Richards (11)

Christmas Night

C loudy, snowy, wet night
H overing with a glitter surprise
R ound about Santa goes, here to there to everywhere
I can see his lovely reindeer flying like a diamond in the air
S o the two of them have a happy time
T aking presents to good kids
M agic is a wonderful sight in the light
A nd be a good person so you'll get nice presents
S ay sorry to a bad thing, it's a nice thing to do

N ightingale's voice can be heard
'I m and Santa are really nice so they listen to the tune
G lowing moon and stars shine
H olding magic that is fine
T ime to go for Santa to disappear in a thin breeze.

Safouana Ahmed (10)

Santa's Saturday Night

Ho! Ho! Ho! Merry Christmas,
Santa Claus is coming on his sleigh.
It's packed full of toys,
'I want them,' all the children say.

Santa wears a tomato-red coat
And has a snowy beard.
Black boots he wears on his feet,
He is strong and has never feared.

His factory is packed,
With lots of little elves.
Making toys is fun for them
And they enjoy building shelves.

As Santa packs his gifts,
There's a full moon tonight,
The children tucked up in beds,
Having dreams and sleeping tight.

Reindeer flying in the sky,
Getting very hungry.
Thump! Santa has landed,
Rudolph says, 'Get a carrot for me.'

As Santa gets to the bottom of the chimney,
He gobbles the mince pies,
He finds a carrot
And writes his goodbyes.

Santa flies back up the chimney,
On the sleigh.
Rudolph gets his carrot,
Santa's on his way.

Zachary Budde (11)

Thank You Santa

Thank you Santa for all my toys,
Thank you from all the girls and boys,
I leave you my mince pies,
So you can fly high in the sky,
And thank you for granting all my Christmas wishes.

Sophie Tullett (8)

For Christmas

Dear Santa,

For Christmas I would like ...
A PlayStation 2,
A pair of new shoes,
A new hot-water bottle,
A brother that doesn't squabble,
A sister that shares,
A new backpack
From out of your sack
And that's all I can think of,
So if I think of more
I'll send you another letter.

Love
Shauna.

PS I would also like to meet you.
PSS I would also like to meet Rudolph.

Shauna Matthews (10)

Christmas Time

S   is for snow slithering down my back
A   is for antlers on the top of Rudolph's head
     like a GPS cable guiding him through the snow
N   is for nuts in the bowl to chomp on ravenously
T   is for tinsel glimmering at me as if I were special
A   is for acting in your Christmas play.

John Loydall (11)

The Night Before Christmas

Father Christmas is coming tonight,
Don't forget to be good and sleep tight.
As we are tucked up in bed fast asleep,
Father Christmas will get all his good treats!
Red wine and mince pies, oh what a surprise,
As Father Christmas and his reindeer fly through the night sky.

I cannot wait until morning to see what he's brought,
I hope Father Christmas has had some good thoughts.
We have got to wait until morning to see what he's left,
Father Christmas is what makes Christmas the best!

Ben Ireson (10)

Dear Santa

You're entertaining and funny
Warm-hearted and sweet,
Cool but with added skills and attitude,
You're just the person I would like to meet.
You're very fat, like a couple of cats,
But it doesn't matter.
Anyway you couldn't get fatter.
Christmas is near,
Get ready to deliver
Presents to everybody around here.

Corinne Figueira (10)

Christmas!

Christmas is a wonderful time,
Where children see their presents in line.
All bright and coloured, red, gold and blue,
Wrapped with love especially for me and you.

Mum works hard preparing the lunch,
Getting it ready for us to munch.
Turkey, carrots, potatoes and sprouts,
It's sure to be lovely, we have no doubts.

Dinner is over, it's time to play
And entertain our family who have come to stay.
Out come the chocolates and other nice things,
Then the karaoke and Grandma sings!

Dad's full of cheer, lager and beer,
Soon the day will be over and we'll celebrate new year.
12 o'clock comes, hip hip hooray!
Time to start saving for next year's big day!

Bethan Long (11)

Waiting For Santa

I was waiting for Santa in my bed,
In the sky, I thought I saw red,
I went downstairs to see if it was him,
When I got there the light was dim,
I saw Santa eating the cookies I had made,
Left presents under the tree - that's how he paid,
He quickly played a game of darts,
I saw him leave with our Christmas cards,
Ho ho ho, Santa was here,
I'll wait for him again next year.

Samera Iqbal (9)

Santa Claus!

On Christmas Eve, when it's cold and chilly,
Santa grabs his sack and climbs down the chimney.
He's wearing his hat, cold and wet,
Delivering presents, I can't wait to get.
He stacks them up under the tree,
Some for my brother, some for me.
Then he climbs up the chimney and gets in his sleigh,
Eager to get back, before Christmas Day.

Molly Archard (9)

Santa, Santa

Santa, Santa, very, very nice,
Santa, Santa, better than spice.

Santa, Santa, very good man,
Lives in a place colder than a fan.

Santa, Santa, dressed in red,
Brings us presents when we're in bed.

He brings us presents big and small,
Wake up early to open them ... *all!*

Anna Fitzgeorge (8)

Santa

Dear Santa,

For Christmas this year I want:
To say thank you
For all my presents I got last year,
That's all I want for Christmas.

PS You're amazing!

Ellen Counsell (10)

Untitled

Christmas time is very fun,
Presents around for everyone.
Santa's working late at night,
Delivering presents till it's light.
Fill our stockings to the top,
They get so full they might pop.
Snow is laid on the ground,
Hardly any path will be found.
Christmas pudding and our lunch
Eat it all up, *munch, munch, munch.*
Hope you enjoy Christmas time
And hope you enjoy my little rhyme!

Jessica McConkey (10)

Christmas

C hristmas is a very special day
H undreds of people were busily wrapping Christmas presents
R eindeer were stamping their hooves and snorting with impatience
I love Christmas
S hining baubles, tiny animals, Father Christmas and silver stars
all over the Christmas tree
T insel is sparkling all over the Christmas tree
M antelpiece above the fire was a piece of cake and a glass of milk
A ngel on the top of the Christmas tree
S anta brings presents all over the world.

Jordan Mancienne-Ponwaye (10)

My Christmas Tree

It's the fifth of December and I haven't got a tree
So I had to get to the shop quickly
There were all kinds of colours to choose from
Blue, green and red
I can just imagine it right beside my bed
I chose the green one, it has to be the best
It stands out much more from all the rest
I get some decorations, lots and lots of tinsel
I pull it all out of the box and I get into a tangle
I put some more decorations on the tree
But all of a sudden, it was not green
There were so many decorations, the tree was not seen.

Katherine Williams (9)

Santa's Presents

Where are Santa's presents
I wonder what he's got
I can't wait till Christmas
Because I want the lot

Where are Santa's presents
I wonder what he's got
A teddy perhaps ...
Or maybe not

Where are Santa's presents
I wonder what he's got
A ripe apple tree with rosy-red apples
In a beautifully decorated pot.

Elin Shaw (8)

That's Christmas

Santa sees us when we're sleeping,
When we're tucked up in bed
With Christmas thoughts running through our excited heads,
That's Christmas!

I've put out my whisky and pies,
Oh I wish I could see Santa with my own eyes,
That's Christmas!

Wake up, it's morning time,
I've just heard my alarm clock chime,
That's Christmas!

I race downstairs to my Christmas tree,
When all I see is the soot from my chimney,
That's Christmas!

But when I turned around,
Look what I found ...
Presents! Ho, ho, ho,
That's Christmas!

Stephanie Gardner (10)

Santa, Santa Help Me!

Santa, Santa what will you bring?
My dad wants a boat
My mum a diamond ring
My brother wants to fly a plane
My sister wants a phone
But every time I write my list
All they do is moan!
Santa will you help me?
You'll have to help me soon
You see, I want a spaceship
To fly me to the moon!

Michael Reed (11)

Clumsy Santa

You fell down the chimney with a thump,
Presents landed in a hump,
Soot and ashes were on the floor,
Mum should have said, 'Come through the front door!'
Mince pies and wine will be left on the chair,
Next to the sofa right over there.
Fill my stocking to the brim,
Big and bulky - not too thin!

Jade Elizabeth Moulton (11)

Christmas

Robins sitting in the trees,
Snowflakes dancing in the breeze,
A dazzling light from every tree,
Presents are all just for me!

Chloe Lawrence (9)

Santa

Santa comes on Christmas Eve,
Santa comes for you and me,
Santa comes with lots of toys,
Santa comes for girls and boys,
Santa travels round the world,
Santa comes once a year!

Natalie Doggett (9)

Last Day Of Term

Listening to music,
Friends chatting, laughing, having fun!
Christmas cards littering every desk,
Everyone eating cookies, drinking juice.
Christmas just around the corner,
A hubbub of noise.

Silence.
No one there.
Christmas cards vanished.
Crumbs and envelopes dumped in an overflowing bin.
Christmas come and gone.
Silence - except for music,
Still softly playing.

Alice Robinson (11)

Untitled

Santa, Santa please come here
If I see you I will give a loud cheer
With the carrots in the gardens
And mince pies under the tree
Please, please Santa will you visit me?

Kieron Walters (4)

My Name Is Rudolph

My name is Rudolph the reindeer
And I pull Santa's sleigh,
But when we should be working,
We often laugh and play.
But today we have to concentrate
Because when Christmas Day will come,
We have to deliver all the presents
Or else Santa won't get his rum!

Elizabeth Wells

Christmas Is A Day

Christmas is a day
When everybody plays
Christmas is a day
Not in May
Christmas is a day
When horses get more hay
This is Christmas Day

Santa climbs down
With a sack coloured brown
Santa climbs down
With maybe a toy clown
Santa climbs down
Without a sound
This is Christmas Day

This is when the snow falls
This is when my dog gets called
This is when the snow falls
This is when the frost goes on walls
This is when the snow falls
I've got nothing, this is all.

Stacey Parsons (9)

Santa

Every year on the 25th
Santa brings us gifts
Many wonderful things
To find on the magical day
He comes down the chimney
With a sack of toys
For all the girls and boys

When we awake
There is so much to see
So much happiness and glee
We open our presents
Amid laughter and fun
That brings happiness to everyone.

Jack Lewis (10)

Untitled

Waiting for Christmas Day
He's gonna fly his sleigh,
Rudolph at the front leading all the way,
Toys dropped down the chimney,
Ready for girls to play,
Boys are on the naughty list,
They won't have a good day,
While Santa is on his way
Hip hip hooray!

Bethany France (8)

Santa's Coming

As we're warm in our beds
Santa's coming on his sledge

Reindeer glowing in the sky
Pulling Santa very high

Then the reindeer stop and wait
Santa's coming through our gate

Now for the wait!

Lucy Brockway (11)

Dear Santa

I wish that I could see smiles on everyone's faces.
I wish that I could give lonely children
the best gift of all, a family.
I wish that I could help to stop poverty.
All these things that I want for Christmas,
but never so selfish am I.
So all I ask for Christmas this year
is to look over these poor people, Santa for Christmas
and help them to get through the winter season
with a happy face.

Apostolis Poulakis (13)

Santa Claus

S now is really fun to make snowmen with
A utumn comes just before you and scatters colourful crispy leaves
N ow it's time for you to make presents for the children around the world
T hank you for all the hard work you put into Christmas with
   your reindeer too
A ll the presents you give to us we all appreciate

C hristmas crackers make you jump and decorate your family lunch
L apland is where you live, sharing with your wife and elves
A fter Christmas comes, New Year, time for you to celebrate
U nderneath the mistletoe I see you kiss my mam
S o now it is all over you have a year's rest.

Kirsty Ann Washington (10)

In Winter

In winter it is always cold and frosty days,
When children go out and play.
Your mum tells you to wear a scarf and hat,
But if it was me I would put them on the cat.
Some people think building snowmen is the most fun,
But then it will all melt with the sun.
Some look forward to presents and food
And some hate it like Scrooge.

Lydia Wade (9)

All I Want For Christmas ...

All I want for Christmas ...
is a motorbike to ride
'cause I *will* wear a helmet
and ride it round with pride.

Thank you Santa.

All I want for Christmas ...
is a dog to chase and train
and if I put him in a carrier,
I can take him on a plane.

Thank you Santa.

All I want for Christmas ...
is a pony to love and hug
and ride him round the sand school,
with a little pull and tug.

Thank you Santa.

All I really want to have,
to make my Christmas magic
is to have my family around me,
and nothing to be tragic.

Thank you Santa!

Angela Petrassei (9)

Untitled

Santa, Santa
Please drop in
Santa, Santa
Will you fill
My stocking
Up and up to the top?
Fill it up till
It makes me *pop!*

Shannon Lewis (9)

Santa Is Nice

Santa is nice,
Santa is kind,
He gives us presents
At Christmas time.

Santa has reindeer
That fly through the sky,
Santa is the best Christmas guy.

Santa is clever,
Santa is cool,
Santa should rule, that's cool.

Christmas bells ringing,
All people singing,
'Santa is busy tonight.'

Ho, ho, ho, we love Santa,
Ho, ho, ho, we love Santa,
Santa we love you all year through.

Safa Khalil (9)

Chocolate Santa

He is a very jolly chap
A wonderful surprise
He doesn't dance or spin around
Can you see through his disguise?

Underneath his shiny wrapper
Underneath his red and white
He is just a chocolate Santa
A tasty Xmas delight.

Jessica Alice Hirst (10)

Whispers Of Santa Claus

It's the night before Christmas,
Everything's on pause,
All but the excited whispers,
Whispers of Santa Claus.

Whispers of teddies and toys,
Wishes of footballs for boys,
Sweeties and games, CDs and fast trains,
Santa Claus is on his way!

Whispers of clothes from the latest trend,
Wishes of pencils and pens that can bend,
A delicious cake and things to make,
Santa Claus is on his way.

It's the night before Christmas,
Everything's on pause,
All but the excited whispers,
Whispers of Santa Claus.

Isla Cunningham (10)

For Christmas I Would Like ...

For Christmas I would like ...
An everlasting snowball that doesn't melt in your hands
A silver bell that never stops ringing
A stocking filled with a year's supply of toys
A Christmas tree with shining baubles
And tinsel that glimmers in the moonlight
A choir of angels singing so beautifully
That everyone would gather around to listen
A Christmas dinner with a tender juicy turkey
A holly bush with ripe red berries to feed the birds
And a dazzling gold star to light up the whole world.

Hannah Lindley (10)

Guess Who?

I know a man who's one in a million
He wouldn't exchange his job for a billion
He will do anything for us kids
He will buy our baby brothers cribs
He will get through snowy weather
His coat is red leather
I bet you can't guess
He is the best
They call him Santa
Santa the toy maker.

Sophie Waldegrave (11)

Santa It's Christmas!

Santa it's Christmas
Hip hip hooray
Santa it's Christmas
Hip hip hooray

Don't forget to
Drop the presents
Off to all the girls and boys

So they can have
A good Christmas
And you can jump for joy!

Lucy Hammond (11)

Untitled

At Christmas time when we were kids
We all were madly poor,
Santa was quite generous
When he knocked upon my door.

One thing he told me
He wouldn't give money,
Dad horridly said,
'We don't need the money.'

If Rudolph wasn't so lazy
And if Santa wasn't so cuddly,
Santa would get down more chimneys
And deliver more pressies.

Under my Christmas tree
I find a lot of pressies,
Are they from Santa
Or are they from a panda?

Fatima Moosa (8)

Be Good!

To get lots of presents,
You've got to be good,
Great work, great behaviour
Means good presents, good food.

Santa won't come
Unless you're good,
So be smart, don't be dumb,
Don't be rude.

Santa is good,
He lives in the North Pole,
Be good, so you should,
So you won't get a piece of coal!

Heather Perrie (10)

Santa, Santa!

Santa, Santa please come to me,
I have been a good girl you see,
Rudolph will guide you to my house I am sure,
Then come tiptoeing to my door.
Santa, Santa please bring some things,
That dance, prance and sing.
Please leave my presents under the tree,
So when I wake up I awake with glee!

Connie-Mae McCready (10)

Christmas Eve

Santa's coming on Christmas Eve,
With a sack full of toys for you and me.
Jing-a-ling-a-ling the bells cheer,
Watching in the sky where he may appear.
Rudolph's nose red and bright,
Acting as their guiding light.
The sleigh is tipping with the toys,
For all those special little girls and boys.
'Come on Rudolph,' Santa shouts,
'I don't want to miss no kiddie out.'
Thud the sleigh lands on Chloe's house,
But don't be scared 'cause he's about.

Chloe Scrutton (9)

What's Up Santa?

What's up Santa?
Don't be glum,
It's not long till Christmas will come,
Get those elves working,
Prepare your sleigh,
For Christmas is on its way.

What's up Santa?
Don't you fret,
There's nothing left for you to get,
Have a mince pie,
But only one,
For Christmas has just begun.

What's up Santa?
Don't give a sigh,
The stars are all shining brightly in the sky,
Groom all the reindeer, don't pretend,
That your happy Christmas
Has come to an end.

Charlie Emsley (14)

The Christmas Spirit

Christmas tree with lots of lights
People having snowball fights
Mistletoe and dark black nights
Decorations are selling out
Santa is coming
Get ready to shout (ho, ho, ho)
Drink and food here tonight
Remembering Jesus and his plight
Children starting to count down
Everyone being loud
Children filled with joy and cheer
Parents sitting drinking beer
Family greetings on all night
Fireworks being set alight
Now sleep in your bed nice and tight.

Emma Warwood (9)

A Christmas Adventure

I am going on an adventure tonight
I am going with Santa on a flight
Over each house we will fly
Dropping off the pressies as we go by
It is going to be so much fun
Gliding over the hidden sun
And then when Santa
Drops me back into my bed
I will wake up next morning
And unwrap my ted
That was the best night of my life
It would seem
It is such a shame
It was all a dream.

Zoe Warwood (11)

Christmas

Crunchy cookies
Singing carollers
Tasty turkey
Lots of wrapping paper
Christmas is the best.

Aaron Trott (10)

The Man In Red

I love Christmas, the magic of it all
I love the glistening snow
The laughter of children at the pantomime show
Carol singers singing merrily on high
Robin redbreast's red rosy glow
In temperatures of 10 below
Everywhere people laugh and smile
They shout, 'It'll be soon Christmas Day
Have you children been good?
Are you all in a happy mood?'

The best thing about Christmas
Is awaiting the man in red
The presents he leaves at the bottom of your bed
That special toy you wished for
Dad created a special place for it in the shed
Yes, your very own sled
Now you'll go and build a snowman
Before returning home to open your other presents
That the man in red brought in his sack
Cannot wait until next Christmas when he'll be back.

Ciara McDermott (11)

Christmas Morn

As I wake up on Christmas morn
I stare out of my misty window
A crystal white sheet of snow
Covers the icy grass like a silk glove
My excited mind is drawn to a bulging sack
Of delicately wrapped presents
Lots of special surprises fill my imaginative mind
I creep silently down the steep wooden stairs
All that remains of the tasty mince pies and the warm rum feast
Is a few glitter-like crumbs
And a drop of the delicious rum
I can smell the hot smoky fire
It crackles and pops continuously
Carefully I run my finger around the chocolatey Yule log
And scoop it into my mouth
I sneak back up the creaky stairs tenuously
And snuggle down in my heavenly bed
I begin to dream about the mouth-watering feast that awaits me
And I gradually drift back to sleep.

Georgia Wiseman (12)

Santa

S now falling from above the sky
A nd Santa having his midnight feast
N ight-time all the children sleeping tight
T insel dangling from the Christmas tree
A ngels inspiring to lustre the light of the *Lord*.

Mariam Alauddin (11)

The Christmas Child

A royal child was born this day,
In a manger filled with hay.

Ox and ass bowed down before Him,
Shepherds came to adore Him.

A silver star led the way,
For three kings to where he lay.

The kings arrived in coats of fur,
Gifts they gave, gold, frankincense and myrrh.

The angels sang and shone with light,
About the Prince born that night.

Eleanor Westwood (9)

Santa is Coming

Santa Claus is here
So shout out Christmas cheer
All the lights are shining bright
On a snowy Christmas night
Putting the star on top of the tree
Everyone's shouting out with glee
Merry Christmas to you all
Hope you have a Christmas ball.

Nicole Mill (11)

Christmas

C hildren playing all day long
H appy people singing songs
R eindeer galloping in the snow
I vy winding round the stove
S anta nearly on his way
T ime clocks ringing on display
M erry Christmas to you all
A ll the wrapping presents done
S o sing along and have some fun!

Iman Jamil (8)

Naughty Or Nice?

This year I have been really nice,
except for when I threw the rice
and when I played knock and run
and when I slapped Mum on the bum
and when I lost my friend's toy car
and when I broke my dad's guitar,
but I've really tried to be good,
please bring me pressies ...
I think you should!

Connor Rogers (11)

Untitled

Dear Santa please
Visit me
And leave my presents
Under the tree
We haven't got a chimney
So you will need the magic key
But Rudolph's bright red nose
Will help you see
Thank you, Santa, for coming here
I wish you the best
Happy New Year.

Declan Walters (6)

Christmas Poem

Santa's hat has fallen off
and now old Santa's got a cough.

What's worse is that the elves are scared of working
all because Jack Frost is lurking.

Will the prezzies get out today
or will the kids wait until May?

Rudolph's got a trick up his sleeve
but first Jack Frost has got to leave.

The elves design a water gun
and shoot Jack Frost in the bum.

Cold old Jack begins to melt,
the elves' deed has now been dealt.

The prezzies are out by morning
just as the sun is dawning.

Thanks to Rudolph's quest
this Christmas is the best!

Keelan Smith-Evans (12)

Young Writers Information

We hope you have enjoyed reading this book - and that you will continue to enjoy it in the coming years.

If you like reading and writing poetry and short stories drop us a line, or give us a call, and we'll send you a free information pack.

Alternatively, if you would like to order further copies of this book or any of our other titles, then please give us a call or log onto our website at **www.youngwriters.co.uk**

Young Writers, Remus House, Coltsfoot Drive, Woodston, Peterborough PE2 9JX

Tel (01733) 890066

Email youngwriters@forwardpress.co.uk